Unburied

Unburied

Latasha Schaller

IGUANA

Copyright © 2022 Latasha Schaller
Published by Iguana Books
720 Bathurst Street, Suite 303
Toronto, ON M5S 2R4

Publisher: Meghan Behse
Cover design: Jonathan Relph
Front cover image: MAYSHOillusto via stock.adobe.com

ISBN 978-1-77180-552-0 (paperback)
ISBN 978-1-77180-551-3 (epub)

This is an original print edition of *Unburied*.

To my husband —

Thank you for loving the broken parts of me
that I was trying to hide.

"I told him I believed in hell, and that certain people, like me, had to live in hell before they died, to make up for missing out on it after death, since they didn't believe in life after death, and what each person believed happened to him when he died."

— Sylvia Plath, *The Bell Jar*

"There is something at work in my soul, which I do not understand."

— Mary Shelley, *Frankenstein*

Trapped

I do
not
know
where to begin

There are so many

beginnings
& endings
endings
& beginnings

I have
become
untethered
ungrounded

I

saw myself
understood myself
created myself

in relation to
things
people
places
that I can
no longer claim,

&
no longer
be claimed by

II

I feel
like I
do not
belong
in this world

(why else
would I feel
this way)

Why else
would I feel
without direction
without purpose
without belief
in my
own
future?

III

I feel
at
odds with
evolution—

because
what
evolutionary
sense
does
my mind
make

what
evolutionary
purpose
does a mind
that
folds in
on
itself
serve

IV

But —
of course
this is
more than
evolution

We are advancing
faster
than
evolution

We are
going
beyond
the limits
of humanity

& our
delicate minds
cannot
take
it

V

I do
not
know
what to do
with all
of this
pain
anger
sadness
inside of me

I do
not
know
why
it is there,
or where
it comes from

Is it because of
what has happened
to me
by me
in spite of me?

Or is it just
who I am?

What makes
me,
me?

At what
point
will I
stop asking

& start
accepting?

VI

I can never
flee from
myself

(*my mind*)

& I can never
truly overcome
it

VII

To wish
you had
never been
born
is different
than wishing
you were
dead

But —
does that
make it
any
better?

L'appel du vide

It is
not
the fear
of falling

but
the fear
of wanting

(the *desire*)

to jump
that
scares
me

to death

IX

I would rather
sound
crazy
than
afraid

I would rather
scream
out
my pain
than
hide it
away

X

Accepting that
I *was* broken
is easier than
accepting that
I *am* broken

—

how can a
fractured
mind repair
itself?

XI

Is it the
act of breaking
that is
so damaging

or

is it the
realization
that
you are
not

(& may have never been)

whole

XII

Who am I
to pretend
to be
superior
when it comes
to the parts
of
my fractured
mind

How can I
cling to
the rational

& willfully pretend
the irrational
is not
also me

— when it is
simply
the part
of myself
that I choose
not

to claim

XIII

I must
take
ownership of
my mind
before it begins
to own
me

XIV

At what
point
will
I stop
identifying
with my

fears
anxieties
insecurities

& realize
that I cannot
define
myself
by the parts of
myself
that I hide?

Because
that
is exactly
what gives
them
power

XV

At what
point
does the

grasping
clinging
tethering

to all
those
years of

pain
anger
sadness

stop

At what
point
is it up to
me
to

let go
move on
accept

that which has
happened

~~to~~

~~me~~

XVI

I do not
have
a lot of faith
that others
will
not

let me down
run away
leave

& I
blame **you**
for
that

XVII

I should not
have
had to
make
excuses
for you

But
what other
choice
did
I have?

XVIII

Pain is a
patchwork-quilt

handed down —
owned
but never
claimed

the only
comfort
it allows
is the
knowledge
of its
path
through
your family
to you
in this

darkness

that
you
share

& you,
who decide
to put it
outside,

on the line —

to be
seen
warmed
destroyed
by its movement
into
the
light —

the sun
piercing holes,
wearing away
years of
resentment
bitterness
heartache

till nothing remains —

apart from
the vision
burned
into your
mind's
eye

This Cycle is Repetitive

When it comes to
the mind
it is not merely an

imbalance
of
chemicals

or a
difficult
warped
traumatic
childhood —

it is both,

& so
much
more —

it is
an endlessly
repeating
cycle

& the irony
is that the
only way to
stop it,
is to
end
it

(**this** is what I want
to tell you,
when you ask why

I
am
not
having
kids)

XX

We are made to
believe
that

who we are
is who
they were

meant to be
tried to be
could not be

We must be
better
richer
more accomplished —

to make
this
all
worth it

(for them)

XXI

It is insurmountable —

the *name,*
the *burden,*
the *legacy* —

to pay
not for the sin
but for
the greatness —

to feel as if
my life
has to make up
for the
brevity
of his —

the
long end
to a
short life

XXII

To identify
one's self —

to understand
one's
personality
drives
desires

in relation to an
unknown ideal

is damaging

To accept a part of
one's self
as unknowable is

detrimental
to the

soul

Was I Meant to Be Born (With This *Mind)*

Someone
must pay
the price

for *love*
for *desire*
for *taking*

that which
nature
did
not
grant

—

did
not
willingly
give

At what point will we
ask, not
can we
do this,
but
should we

What does it mean
to create
when we have
stolen
the tools for that
creation
from nature

Herself

XXIV

Perhaps
it is

this *fracturing*
this *ripping*

of the
unready soul
from
the
universe

& forcing it

into reality
that causes all
of this

dysfunction
& mental damnation

XXV

Part
of me
always knew

that things
did not
feel right —

that there was

some *disconnect*
some *reason*

I felt
othered
outsided
outcast

Does
a soul know
when it is
living
a
lie?

XXVI

They say
blood
is
thicker
than
water —

But why does this allow
pain
abuse
mistreatment
to be
excused
understood
explained

How does
familiarity
justify
cruelty

How do
family ties
justify
silence

Why does
blood
signify
repression

XXVII

What happens
when family
ties are
cut

When you
allow yourself
to be
unclaimed
unchained
unchanged

by who
they are,

by who
they want

you

to be?

XXVIII

Why
do
we place
our value
in the hands
of those
who we
do not trust
to show
our true
selves?

XXIX

Why
am I
to blame
for my sudden

(been coming for years)

refusal
to accept
the
bullshit
that you
call
love?

XXX

Do not
begrudge me
the strength

to be
who
I am

just because you
are too weak
to do the
same

XXXI

What if
self-acceptance
is just the
rejection
of those who
believe that
they
created
you

XXXII

I am
two
selves

I live in
two
worlds

between

who
I *know* that
I am

&

who
you *believe* me
to be

XXXIII

I
am not
changed
by what
you think
of me

You can
only affect the
me
that exists
within
you

& she
is a
stranger
to me

XXXIV

We exist
in *many minds*
in *many stories*
in *many lives*

We are each
imagined
rewritten
changed
to fit

our place
in another
person's
life

We
become
who they
want
need
desire
us to be

XXXV

The trick
is to not let any
of *them*
define
you

XXXVI

Where
do I
find myself?

Is it in
the *becoming*
of who
I am

or

Is it in
the *accepting*
of who
I have

always

been?

XXXVII

Am I

just a
collection
of stories
left untold

just a
collection
of scars
that never
healed

just a
collection
of words
left unspoken

Am I
all that
I have done

or

am I
all that
I have left
to
do

XXXVIII

Sometimes
you need

to see *how*

something was
broken
before
you can
fix it

XXXIX

Sometimes
you need

to feel *everything*

in order to
make sense
of
any
of
it

XL

Sometimes
you need

to accept *all*

of those
broken pieces
before
you can
heal
yourself

XLI

Not
all pain
has a lesson

Sometimes
it is
just

another thing

that you
refused
to let
destroy
you

XLII

        I am not
        the girl
    that those things
    happened to —

I am
the woman
who refused
to let them
define
her

My Mind is Papered with Yellow

It is
easier
to blame
the *anxiety*
the *depression*
the *intrusive thoughts*
on

faulty wires
& misfiring chemicals

than it is
to accept
that it is
so
much
more
than that

Because
then I
would have to
hold myself
accountable
rather than
see myself

as the
unwilling
victim

XLIV

There is
a freedom
in knowing
why
you are
the way that
you are

There is
a trap
in believing
that
is all that
you are

I have ____
               but
I am not ____

            I can
acknowledge

            but —

        I will not
           let *it*
         define
            me

XLV

The hardest part
to accept
is that
this
is for life —

that I will
always have
this
voice inside,
telling me

I am *not enough*
I will always *be alone*
I can never *be loved*
for who I am

The Madness Within

I cannot
blame the woman
trapped
in the attic
of my mind
for how
I made her
feel

I tried to
stifle
quiet
ignore
her

I pretended
she was
not
there —

I pretended
she was
not
a
part
of me

I must build
bridges
within
myself
in order to
heal
us
both

XLVII

A mind
divided
can never be
as strong
as a mind
that

acknowledges
accepts
understands

that to
be whole
is to welcome
the parts that
you have
labelled as
broken

XLVIII

My life
will always
be a
fight
acceptance
process

of healing the cracks
within
myself

Paradise Found

It is a
never-
ending
battle
within
my
mind

It is a war
that can

never

be won

&

I am
beginning
to realize

that
maybe
that means
it can also

never

be lost

L

How can I expect
someone else
to accept
me for

what I am

when I
can barely
accept
myself?

Because
maybe
they see
the whole
where
I only see
the parts

that

are

broken—

Because maybe
what they see
is not

blurred
hidden
misunderstood

by the

anxieties
& fears

that cloud
my mind—

Because
maybe
they

understand
accept
acknowledge

who I am
& know that

the continuous

breaking
& mending

is just a part
of what
makes me,
me

LI

It is a
beautiful thing
to

see
understand
appreciate

another's
flaws—

to allow them
to be as

messy
confused
weird

as they are
&
as they need to be

LII

There are
few
things

more powerful

than a
person
soul
partner

who can make
you laugh

when you
do not
even
have
the
energy

to smile

LIII

I do
not know
if your soul
was made
for mine

But —

I can feel the pull
of my soul
to yours

(are they made of the same?)

you

make me
feel alive

My Multitudes Contain Hell

I
feel
everything
so deeply

& for a very
very long time
I saw that
as a curse

Until I realized the

joy
beauty
strength

in holding
such powerful
feelings
within myself

& having
the ability
to *not*
explode

I contain
more power
than
you could
ever
imagine

LV

I may have been
to Hell

but

I have
also
come back

& no matter
how many
times
my soul is
plunged
into that
dark
abyss

I know
that I will
always
fight
my way
out

& be
once more
freed from
that part of

my
mind

LVI

It has
long been
my belief
that

those
of us living
with mental
illness

those
of us who
have *uncontrollable*
thoughts that we
cannot escape —

regardless
of the
pills
treatments
therapies

— were born

out of time
&
out of place

Ars Longa

&
maybe
we have been
using

our words

to create
a world
just
for
us

Vita Brevis

It is those of us
living on

the *edges*
the *borders*
the *in-between*

spaces

who are able
to create

Our world is the liminal —

between

life & death
creation & destruction
beginning & end

We use
our creation
to combat
the constant
annihilation
we feel
within
ourselves

Memento Mori

Maybe those
of us
who create
are able to
do so
because
we
see the
truth
of
this
world

We have seen
behind the curtain

& can
embrace
death
as an
old friend

LX

Maybe those
who create

dark worlds
& darker images

do so to clear

space

in their own minds

to allow the light in

to reveal some essential fear

to reach out to those also in
the dark

Because
everyone
understands
happiness —

but not everyone
understands

the outsider

within,
or the

comfort
fear
shame

that comes with
accepting
the other
as yourself

LXI

Life
might not
always
feel worth
living —

but

I promise you —

the parts
that are,
are

more brilliant
than your
darkened mind

could
ever
imagine

www.ingramcontent.com/pod-product-compliance
Lightning Source LLC
Chambersburg PA
CBHW051736040426
42447CB00008B/1153